*White Buildings*

# WHITE BUILDINGS

*Poems by*

## HART CRANE

*With an Introduction by*
### ALLEN TATE

*And a Foreword by*
### JOHN LOGAN

## LIVERIGHT
*New York*

ISBN: 0-87140-078-2
Library of Congress Catalog Card Number: 72-86643

1.987654321
Liveright Paperbound Edition 1972

Manufactured in the United States of America

*To*
WALDO FRANK

Certain of these poems first appeared in the following magazines: *Broom, The Dial, Double Dealer, Fugitive, Little Review, 1924, Poetry, Secession,* and *The Calendar* (London).

Ce ne peut être que la fin du monde, en avançant.

—RIMBAUD

# CONTENTS

# INTRODUCTION

THE poetry of Hart Crane is ambitious. It is the only poetry I am acquainted with which is at once contemporary and in the grand manner. It is an American poetry. Crane's themes are abstractly, metaphysically conceived, but they are definitely confined to· an experience of the American scene. In such poems as The Wine Menagerie, For the Marriage of Faustus and Helen, Recitative, he is the poet of the complex urban civilization of his age: precision, abstraction, power. There is no *pastiche;* when he employs symbols from traditional literature, the intention is personally symbolic; it is never falsely pretentious with the common baggage of poetical speech, the properties coveted by the vulgar as inherently poetic.

Hart Crane's first experiments in verse are not, of course, collected in this volume, which contains with one or two exceptions only those poems exhibiting the qualities likely to be permanent in his work. Of these exceptions there is the perfectly written piece of Imagism, Garden

Abstract. This poem evinces several properties of the "new poetry" of a decade ago, the merits and the limitations of the Imagists. To the Imagists Crane doubtless went to school in poetry. He learned their structural economy; he followed their rejection of the worn-out poetic phrase; he must have studied the experiments in rhythm of Pound, Aldington, Fletcher. From Pound and Eliot he got his first conception of what it is, in the complete sense, to be contemporary.

But Crane suddenly and profoundly broke with the methods of Imagism, with its decorative and fragmentary world. To the conceptual mind a world set up not by inclusive assertion but by exclusive attention to the objects of sense lacks imaginative coördination; a method which refuses to exceed the dry presentation of *petites sensations* confines the creative vision to suggestions, to implicit indications, but it cannot arrive at the direct affirmation, of a complete world. A series of Imagistic poems is a series of worlds. The poems of Hart Crane are facets of a single vision; they refer to a central imagination, a single evaluating power, which is at once the motive of the poetry and the form of its realization.

The poet who tries to release the imagination as an integer of perception attempts the solution of the leading contemporary problem of his art. It would be impertinent to enumerate here the underlying causes of the dissociation of the modern consciousness: the poet no longer apprehends his world as a Whole. The dissociation appears decisively for the first time in Baudelaire. It is the separation of vision and subject; since Baudelaire's time poets have in some sense been deficient in the one or the other. For the revolt of Rimbaud, in this distinction, was a repudiation of the commonly available themes of poetry, followed by a steady attenuation of vision in the absence of thematic control. Exactly to the extent to which the ready-made theme controls the vision, the vision is restricted by tradition and may, to that extent, be defined by tradition. In The Waste Land, which revives the essence of the problem, Mr. Eliot displays vision and subject once more in traditional schemes; the vision for some reason is dissipated, and the subject dead. For while Mr. Eliot might have written a more ambitiously unified poem, the unity would have been false; tradition as unity is not contemporary. The important contemporary poet has the rapidly diminishing privilege of reorganizing the subjects of the past. He must construct and assimilate his own subjects. Dante had only to assimilate his.

If the energy of Crane's vision never quite reaches a sustained maximum, it is because he has not found a suitable theme. To realize even partially, at the present time, the maximum of poetic energy demonstrates an important intention. Crane's poems are a fresh vision of the world, so intensely personalized in a new creative language that only the strictest and most unprepossessed effort of attention can take it in. Until vision and subject completely fuse, the poems will be difficult. The comprehensiveness and lucidity of any poetry, the capacity for poetry being assumed as proved, are in direct proportion to the availability of a comprehensive and perfectly articulated given theme.

Crane wields a sonorous rhetoric that takes the reader to Marlowe and the Elizabethans. His blank verse, the most sustained medium he controls, is pre-Websterian; it is measured, richly textured, rhetorical. But his spiritual allegiances are outside the English tradition. Melville and Whitman are his avowed masters. In his sea poems, Voyages, in Emblems of Conduct, in allusions to the sea throughout his work, there is something of Melville's intense, transcendental brooding on the mystery of the "high interiors of the sea." I do not know whether he has mastered Poe's criticism, yet some of his conviction that the poet should be intensely local must stem from Poe. Most of it, however, he undoubtedly gets from Whitman. Whitman's range was possible in an America of prophecy; Crane's America is materially the same, but it approaches a balance of forces; it is a realization; and the poet, confronted with a complex present experience, gains in intensity what he loses in range. The great proportions of the myth have collapsed in its reality. Crane's poetry is a concentration of certain phases of the Whitman substance, the fragments of the myth.

The great difficulty which his poetry presents the reader is the style. It is possible that his style may check the immediate currency of the most distinguished American poetry of the age, for there has been very little preparation in America for a difficult poetry; the Imagistic impressionism of the last ten years has not supplied it. Although Crane is probably not a critical and systematic reader of foreign literatures, his French is better than Whitman's; he may have learned something from Laforgue and, particularly, Rimbaud; or something of these poets from Miss Sitwell, Mr. Wallace Stevens, or Mr. T. S. Eliot.

He shares with Rimbaud the device of oblique presentation of theme. The theme never appears in explicit statement. It is formulated through a series of complex metaphors which defy a paraphrasing of the sense into an equivalent prose. The reader is plunged into a strangely unfamiliar *milieu* of sensation, and the principle of its organization is not immediately grasped. The *logical* meaning can never be derived (see Passage, Lachrymae Christi); but the *poetical* meaning is a direct intuition, realized prior to an explicit knowledge of the subject-matter of the poem. The poem does not *convey;* it *presents;* it is not topical, but expressive.

There is the opinion abroad that Crane's poetry is, in some indefinite sense, "new." It is likely to be appropriated by one of the several esoteric cults of the American soul. It tends toward the formation of a state of mind, the critical equivalent of which would be in effect an exposure of the confusion and irrelevance of the current journalism of poetry, and of how far behind the creative impulse the critical intelligence, at the moment, lags. It is to be hoped, therefore, that this state of mind, where it may be registered at all, will not at its outset be shunted into a false context of obscure religious values, that a barrier will not be erected between it and the rational order of criticism. For, unless the present critic is deceived as to the structure of his tradition, the well-meaning criticism since Poe has supported a vicious confusion: it has transferred the states of mind of poetry from their proper contexts to the alien contexts of moral and social aspiration. The moral emphasis is valid; but its focus on the consequences of the state of mind, instead of on its properties as art, has throttled a tradition in poetry. The moral values of literature should derive from literature, not from the personal values of the critic; their public circulation in criticism, if they are not ultimately to be rendered inimical to literature, should be controlled by the literary intention. There have been poetries of "genius" in America, but each of these as poetry has been scattered, and converted into an *impasse* to further extensions of the same order of imagination.

A living art is new; it is old. The formula which I have contrived in elucidation of Crane's difficulty for the reader (a thankless task, since the difficulty inheres equally in him) is a formula for most romantic poetry. Shelley could not have been influenced by Rimbaud, but he wrote this "difficult" verse:

*Pinnacled dim in the intense inane.*

The present faults of Crane's poetry (it has its faults: it is not the purpose of this Foreword to disguise them) cannot be isolated in a line-by-line recognition of his difficulty. If the poems are sometimes obscure, the obscurity is structural and deeper. His faults, as I have indicated, lie in the occasional failure of meeting between vision and subject. The vision often strains and overreaches the theme. This fault, common among ambitious poets since Baudelaire, is not unique with them. It appears whenever the existing poetic order no longer supports the imagination. It appeared in the eighteenth century with the poetry of William Blake.

ALLEN TATE

*1926*

# FOREWORD

In October 1925 Hart Crane wrote to one of his closest friends, the Cleveland painter William Sommer:

> I know you'll be glad to know that there is a good chance of my first book of poems, *White Buildings,* being published by next spring. In fact Boni and Liveright (at Waldo Frank's persuasion) have practically agreed to bring it out if Eugene O'Neill will consent to write a short foreword. They have lost so much money on the better kind of poetry (which simply doesn't sell these days) that they want to hook the book up with an illustrious name and catch the public that way as much as possible.

Publishing has not changed since that time as far as sales of "the better kind of poetry" are concerned. But the size of Hart Crane's audience has changed dramatically for the better and so has the magnitude of critical attention paid to him—there are some sixty pages of references to critical articles on Crane in David C. Clark's unpublished "Checklist of Hart Crane." How good and useful, then, to have Crane's beautiful first book available in a separate paperback edition. It is a book which he himself was to say contained perhaps his soundest work.

In fact, though O'Neill agreed to do the foreword (and at one time Crane was under the impression that he had finished it), he did not do it. The playwright was enthusiastic about the poetry, but he could not say why, not being "a critic of poetry."

Crane wrote his mother in late July of the following year that the book had indeed been accepted and that "None other than Allen Tate it seems is to write the foreword." He added that—through what seems to me an extraordinary act of generosity—deferring to the greater reputation of the playwright, Tate offered *his* foreword under the name of O'Neill. But Crane himself would not hear of this and ended his letter by saying that "my umbrage toward Allen is erased by the fidelity of his action, and I'm glad to have so discriminating an estimate as he will write of me." That "umbrage" had grown from the strain of the attempts of Crane and the Tates to share a house together, a strain which is perhaps caught most clearly in Tate's later statement that Crane "turned to his friends for the totally committed love, the disinterested *caritas,* that only one's family can sustain."

The first edition of *White Buildings* (the title was taken from a line of one of its poems, "Recitative") appeared in December 1926 with Tate's signed foreword, an apocalyptic epigraph from Rimbaud, whose work and aesthetics Crane so much admired, and a dedication to Waldo Frank, who not only had been his dear friend and correspondent for a long time but who had also done so much to help get these poems published.

It is an astonishing fact that in the *New York Times* obituary of Waldo Frank in the issue of January 10, 1967, there was not a single mention of the name of Hart Crane. Is it possible that the writer of the obituary found the name of Crane unsavoury and was being protective of Frank? There is no doubt that many teachers and readers of poetry found it so earlier—and even recently, as is indicated, for example, by the absurdly bad review of John Unterecker's superb ten year labor of love, *Voyager: A Life of Hart Crane* (1969), in *Poetry*, ironically one of Crane's earliest and most faithful publishers. The reviewer there wrote that moving through the story of Crane's life he felt "soiled by dark secrets which I'd rather not possess at all." This is a feeling that many have apparently shared. One of the reasons for this reaction is surely the fact that Crane was bisexual. Commonly thought to be a "straight" homosexual, Crane twice asked women to marry him, first Lorna Dietz and then Peggy Baird Cowley (formerly Mrs. Malcolm Cowley). At the time of his death Crane was engaged to the latter, deeply in love with her, as he wrote various friends, and had been living intimately with her in Mexico.

Except for his relationship with Emil Opfer, the sailor Crane is in part writing about in "Voyages," his closest associations were not homosexual—in fact his dearest friends were for the most part married couples. He delighted in the company of women. Opfer himself was bisexual rather than homosexual and later married and raised a family. Crane tended to dislike the "gay" scene and wrote once after having left such a scene in California, "I never could stand too much falsetto, you know."

I dwell on this motif of *bi*sexuality in Crane's life and work, first, because the biographical fact of it in his case helps to account for the difficulty his poetry had in being accepted by an earlier generation, a difficulty which was compounded by an obscurity sometimes present in the language. This obscurity is due in part to the fact that Crane felt compelled to hide and/or to transform his sexuality in his language, and in part due to a then avant garde symbolist or surrealist mode of expression.

Second, I dwell on this motif because in *White Buildings,* more than in any other first-rate American poetry (the possible exception would be Whitman), there is so much to be learned—beneath, or through, the extraordinary beauty of the work— about the dynamics of human sexuality, particularly about the balancing of feminine and masculine aspects of the personality. This balancing is now increasingly recognized as part of a universal human need. Poets have always shown their awareness of bisexual feeling through creation myths like that of Plato's Aristophanes in the *Symposium,* through the embodiment of mythological figures such as the androgynous Tiresias, or indeed directly, as in Whitman's "self." Recent biology and depth psychology (most notably Jung) have tried to make clearer this implicit discovery of poetry.

I do not wish to suggest that either the biological or the psychological grounds of bisexual disposition have been discovered *since* Hart Crane wrote. They were of course known before (it's not clear, incidentally, whether Crane ever read either Freud or Jung). The general acceptance of them was slow because of the anxieties the knowledge of them rouses and because of the antisocial actions the conflicts generated by these anxieties sometimes lead to. We are now more open to the universal ground of bisexuality, and therefore to Hart Crane's work, and we can be more grateful for his expression, in some of the most moving poetry ever written in English, of the bisexual aspect of the interior life, particularly of its integration there. Not that this is the only or even the principal matter of Crane's work, but it is a too long neglected aspect.

Since there *is* a problem of balancing the masculine and the feminine elements in order to discover and develop one's own identity, there is usually a conflict. It is one which Crane felt painfully.

Through his poetry, then, in Lionel Trilling's words, he "expresses the pain we all feel."

It is a conflict Crane finally felt tragically, for he committed suicide on his return from Mexico to be married in April 1932, at the end of a long period of vacillation. During a drunken night Crane apparently sought out men aboard the returning ship, and perhaps did so (the facts are unclear) when he missed (through her going to the wrong place) a meeting with his fiancée in Havana the previous day. He continually and drunkenly sought her out that afternoon and evening after their separate reboarding. Peggy Cowley, upset at his not meeting her and at Crane's drinking, and having suffered on her return to the ship a painful injury from exploding matches, had little patience with Crane. After finishing a huge breakfast on his final morning, Crane went to Peggy's cabin still in his pajamas, unshaven, dejected from his experiences of the night before, during which he had been beaten and robbed, and sat beside her on her berth. When she insisted that he get shaved and dressed (it was nearly noon), he left. He went to the stern deck rail of the ship, which he had been wrestled away from once the night before, already in despair. He carefully folded and placed on the deck the raincoat he had been wearing as a robe over his pajamas, balanced on the rail, leaped, and went to bed in the sea, waving once goodnight before he sank.

In 1926, as though praying that he might fight off the desire to end the pain of his conflict until he had finished more work, he wrote in the magnificent "Atlantis" section of what was to be *The Bridge:* "Hold thy floating singer late." The singer was held "floating" for a few years more; then, just three months short of age thirty-three, he sank.

Hart Crane balanced on the deck rail as he had tried to balance in his life and work. Unhappily, he failed in life. The poetry, however, is controlled by words as the medium of balance; and words, put together by the gift of the poet to make the architecture of poetry, find a higher realization beyond the drives and ambivalent feelings of the poet's unbalanced sexuality. It is this transcendence which we feel as beauty, and one of its characteristics, one of the gifts of art, is the momentary freedom from the kind of acute anxiety that eventually killed Hart Crane.

Looking for the masculine-feminine balance in the imagery of poems in *White Buildings,* we find two early works (1920) of special interest: "My Grandmother's Love Letters" and "Garden Abstract." The former was the first poem Crane was paid for (ten dollars), and he said this made him feel "literary." He also felt that it was a poem "in an entirely new vein," and he wrote of it, "I don't want to make the dear old lady too sweet or too naughty and balancing on the fine line between these two qualities is going to be fun." I think he means the problem of balancing an over-feminine quality, "sweetness," with an over-masculine one (because over-aggressive), "naughtiness." More to the point, it is clear that he identified the poem itself and his own personality with that of the grand-mother figure.

Crane was living with his grandmother when he began his poem. To show the identification of the poem with his grandmother, there is his remark in a reply to Gorham Munson, "I enjoyed your letter with its encouragement to Grandma and am sending you a record of her behavior to date. She would get very fretful and peevish at times, and at other times hysterical and sentimental." He is speaking of the poem, not the woman. As for his identification with the person of the poem, it is made in the lovely finished version (italics mine):

> And I ask myself
> Are your fingers long enough to play
> Old keys that are but echoes:
> Is the silence strong enough
> To carry back the music to its source
> *And back to you again*
> *As though to her?*

The italicized phrase identifies the grandmother and the writer. I would add that the line "Are your fingers long enough to play" is a questioning about potency in the double sense of sexuality and poetry. Crane's beautiful poem answers affirmatively its own question.

There is a displacement, in Crane's poetry, of the language of the body to the language of the landscape (as in the phrase, "the loose girdle of soft rain"). Although such displacement (one kind of metaphor) is general in poetry, one might find a hint in the particular appearance of it in this "grandmother" poem that Hart Crane's overt homosexuality is in part a defense against admitting the physical feeling for the grandmother or surrogate mother. Certainly the male poet is concerned here with close feeling for the feminine, and perhaps personally with the homosexual aspect of his own bisexual feeling. He appears to believe he might want to share this feeling but that he should in fact hide it from his grandmother, or from the mother if the one can be taken as a figure for the other, for the poem concludes with the stanza,

> Yet I would lead my grandmother by the hand
> Through much of what she would not
>     understand;
> And so I stumble. And the rain continues on
>     the roof
> With such a sound of gently pitying laughter.

(It is worth remembering that Crane did later, rather disastrously, reveal his homosexual feelings to his mother.) In the concluding passage the word "stumble" (lose power) relates to the question "Are your fingers long enough?" (powerful enough). When one remembers the poet's identification with the grandmother one sees that he is carrying on a dialogue with himself about masculine-feminine polarity. The last line avoids self-pity and succeeds in achieving self-compassion. The poem itself does attain balance and thus allays anxiety—provides "catharsis" or what Dylan Thomas called "temporary peace."

"Garden Abstract," which Crane was working on at the same time, is directly pertinent to the theme of bisexual balance, because in it Crane changes the central figure of the poem from a masculine to a feminine one. The first line, "The apple on its bough is her desire," originally read "my desire." Of course it would be possible to argue that "my" represents the persona of a girl from the first. We would then be dealing with a feminine role assumed by the male poet. In earlier poems Crane more than once shifted from "my" to the feminine third person. At any rate Crane reworked the poem considerably, as he tells us in a letter to a friend who had criticized the earlier version as "phallic." The poem begins with a balance in the first two lines of a feminine image ("apple") against a masculine one ("sun") and speaks of the act of balancing ("suspension"). "The apple on its bough is her desire, — / Shining suspension, mimic of the sun."

The word "mimic" therefore has the fascinating suggestion, which we will want to follow up, that the feminine is a metaphor for the masculine.

In the course of the poem the girl is transformed into a tree—in Crane's words, "She comes to dream herself the tree"—and therefore, having lost the sense of herself, "She has no memory, nor fear, nor hope/ Beyond the grass and shadows at her feet." The loss of sense of self is ecstatic ("The wind possessing her"), and we discover ourselves in the presence of an archetypal masculine-feminine transformation which many poets have written about—Petrarch, Rilke, Yeats, Pound, and James Wright, among others—and which the poet Ovid speaks of in his story about the metamorphosis of Daphne. The tree is a sexual symbol that is ambiguous, depending on its context either masculine or feminine, for the trunk and bole of the tree together appear phallic, but its wood, material for making, and its fruitfulness suggest the feminine.

I believe that behind the impulse to write lies the attempt, for the male writer, to feel his way into the world of women, and very likely the reverse is true for the female writer. In his poetry, generally, Hart Crane has much to tell us about this. "Garden Abstract" is a poem about poetry itself, for the girl's (the poet's) voice becomes "dumbly articulate in the slant and rise/ Of branch on branch above her . . ." The branches seen above form, as it were, figures for the alphabet, the writer's tool. Also behind the impulse to write is the wish to feel one's identification with nature, to end one's exile from it. That impulse is satisfied by this poem, with the girl's identification with the tree. There is no doubt that these two impulses (feeling one's way into the world of woman and feeling one's way into the world of nature) are connected in the unconscious/consciousness of the male writer, for after all woman, besides being person, is a part of nature.

Another poem in *White Buildings,* written two years later than "Grandmother" and "Garden Abstract," where apples appear again as feminine and in which feminine imagery is balanced again with masculine is "Sunday Morning Apples." The poem is dedicated to William Sommer and describes a painting of his. It was written, Crane says in a letter to Munson, "out of sheer joy," and it is possible that the last line, "The apples, Bill, the apples!" associates the masculine figure of the friend with that which is sexually attractive to the poet, and thus the feminine aspect also appears, for the word "Bill" can be either nominative of address or a word in apposition to "apples." The poem twice uses orgasmic adjectives, "bursting" and "explosion," the latter occurring just before the final line, and it is filled with balanced sexual imagery.

In the poem the female nude Sommers had drawn is first described with an adjective reminiscent of apples ("ripe"). In that ripe nude with head reared/ Into a realm of swords, her purple shadow/ Bursting in the winter of the world." The feminine figure is associated with the masculine sword while "the purple shadow," which suggests pubic hair, is prefigured by the word "fleece" in the second line. The imagery is balanced too in the final stanza, where it is suggested that the apples be put "beside a pitcher [feminine] with a knife [masculine]."

This is also a poem about poetry, for it speaks of the sexual mystery together with the attempt to inquire into it as being at the source of art: "I have seen the apples that *toss you secrets*/ Beloved apples of seasonable madness/ That *feed your inquiries* with aerial wine." (Italics mine.) Furthermore, it identifies the painter's strength with that of the poet through the phrase "your rich and faithful strength of line." Finally, the poem speaks in simple diction and moves eloquently, dealing as well as any poem in *White Buildings* with the bisexual balancing I speak of, and it images this balancing itself in the phrase "straddling/ Spontaneities that form their independent orbits." Incidentally, the imagery of whiteness is echoed in this poem as in two other poems I write of here, "Grandmother's Love Letters" and "Voyages."

The most ambitious poems in *White Buildings* are "For the Marriage of Faustus and Helen" and "Voyages." I consider the Voyage sequence the greatest achievement in the book and one of the transcendent glories of American literature, and I wish to conclude this Foreword by speaking of it in connection with the motif of bisexual imagery.

Crane wrote his mother in late 1924, "I'm engaged in writing a series of six sea poems called 'Voyages' (they are also love poems)." We know that the primary figure of Crane's love in the poem was the Norwegian sailor Emil Opfer, of whom he wrote to Waldo Frank in a very moving letter:

> For many days, now, I have gone about quite dumb with something for which "happiness" must be too mild a term. At any rate, my aptitude for communication, such as it ever is!, has been limited to one person alone, and perhaps for the first time in my life (and I can only think that it is for the last, so far is my imagination from the conception of anything more profound and lovely than this love). I have wanted to write you more than once, but it will take many letters to let you know what I mean (for myself, at least) when I say that I have seen the Word made Flesh. I mean nothing less, and I know now that there is such a thing as indestructibility. In the deepest sense, where flesh became transformed through intensity of response to counter-response, where sex was beaten out, where a purity of joy was reached that included tears.

Yet it is essential to notice that although the concept of the "incarnate Word" is echoed twice in those six poems, once in "Voyages IV" (in those very terms) and once in "Voyages VI" ("the imaged Word"), Crane is *not* writing simply of homosexual love or of one person. This is not only because great poetry is *always* written out of deeper, more interior, and more universalized generalized feelings than those addressed to a given human being. (I am far from wanting to put down human relationships in comparison with art—on the contrary I hold them above art.) The gifted poet connects with the feelings of his anonymous audience because he is *not* primarily writing to one person exclusively in a limited, epistolary fashion—a form of writing which in fact produces *bad* poetry. What may be true is that the person in question serves to activate the muse in some way, though not in a *direct* way. For the muse is also interior and somehow always present as an aspect of the poet, whereas the figure who stirs the muse and begins the poem varies—may in fact be either masculine, as Emil Opfer, or feminine, as Crane's grandmother.

In the case of "Voyages" we can be sure that the poem is not simply addressed to Opfer, not only because it *is* great but also because of its chronology and imagery. I say chronology, since the original version of "Voyages I" was called "Poster" and was written and published before Crane met Opfer. Also, though there is no evidence that Opfer rejected Crane in fact, the final poem suggests, in the

[xxxi]

classical mode of great love poems, a rejection by the beloved, with a resignation and a turning to the solace of poetry and beauty: "the imaged word . . . It is the unbetrayable reply/ Whose accent no farewell can know."

I refer to the poem's imagery, because although there is what might be taken as a strong strain of homosexual metaphor in "Voyages I" (for example, "Fondle your shells and sticks," which suggest the masculine genitalia) and in other poems of the sequence as well, still by the time of the meeting of the lovers in "Voyages V" we already know that the love referred to is not simply homosexual. "Voyages II" introduces clear feminine images: "Her vast undinal belly moonward bends," etc.; and "Voyages IV" ends with the line, "The secret oar and petals of *all* love" (italics mine), bisexual or both homosexual and heterosexual love. If one compares the image "oar and petals" of "Voyages V" to "shells and sticks" of "Voyages I" he may see the former also as an image of male genitalia, but it would be difficult to deny that "petals" is a word with strong feminine associations, balanced against the word "oar," and the sense of "all" is undeniable.

"Voyages VI" closes with feminine images such as "the petalled word," "the lounged goddess," and the line "Belle Isle, white echo of the oar!" If "oar" is masculine, its "echo" is feminine, as are the connotations of "Belle." Thus Crane's poem ends in the mood of "the eternal feminine" like some other great works of western literature such as "Faust," "Ulysses," and "The Sound and the Fury," but this "eternal feminine" mood gives what may be called "a generative, upward movement" (suggestive of the presence of its opposite) at the end of such works because it is integrated beautifully with "the eternal masculine."

The movement from the sexually masculine through the sexually feminine culminates in "Voyages" in something which, containing both, is higher than either. In Crane's words, "sex is beaten out." The achievement of balance between masculine and feminine imagery inside the poems of Crane is symbolic of the integration of masculine with feminine elements in the human personality and of the transcendence of sexuality. There is in such poetry a transformation of what is grounded in sexuality into something else which is perhaps best called spirituality, or in Rudolf Otto's term, used so effectively by Erik Erikson, "the numinous." Adult human experience thus realizes in a deeply fulfilling way, and at a higher level, the primal peace of the infant, who does not distinguish the sexually opposite father and mother.

JOHN LOGAN
*1972*

# White Buildings

# LEGEND

As silent as a mirror is believed
Realities plunge in silence by . . .

I am not ready for repentance;
Nor to match regrets.   For the moth
Bends no more than the still
Imploring flame.   And tremorous
In the white falling flakes
Kisses are,—
The only worth all granting.

It is to be learned—
This cleaving and this burning,
But only by the one who
Spends out himself again.

Twice and twice
(Again the smoking souvenir,
Bleeding eidolon!) and yet again.

Until the bright logic is won
Unwhispering as a mirror
Is believed.

Then, drop by caustic drop, a perfect cry
Shall string some constant harmony,—
Relentless caper for all those who step
The legend of their youth into the noon.

# BLACK TAMBOURINE

THE interests of a black man in a cellar
Mark tardy judgment on the world's closed door.
Gnats toss in the shadow of a bottle,
And a roach spans a crevice in the floor.

Æsop, driven to pondering, found
Heaven with the tortoise and the hare;
Fox brush and sow ear top his grave
And mingling incantations on the air.

The black man, forlorn in the cellar,
Wanders in some mid-kingdom, dark, that lies,
Between his tambourine, stuck on the wall,
And, in Africa, a carcass quick with flies.

# EMBLEMS OF CONDUCT

By a peninsula the wanderer sat and sketched
The uneven valley graves.  While the apostle
   gave
Alms to the meek the volcano burst
With sulphur and aureate rocks . . .
For joy rides in stupendous coverings
Luring the living into spiritual gates.

Orators follow the universe
And radio the complete laws to the people.
The apostle conveys thought through discipline.
Bowls and cups fill historians with adorations,—
Dull lips commemorating spiritual gates.

The wanderer later chose this spot of rest
Where marble clouds support the sea
And where was finally borne a chosen hero.
By that time summer and smoke were past.
Dolphins still played, arching the horizons,
But only to build memories of spiritual gates.

# MY GRANDMOTHER'S LOVE LETTERS

THERE are no stars to-night
But those of memory.
Yet how much room for memory there is
In the loose girdle of soft rain.

There is even room enough
For the letters of my mother's mother,
Elizabeth,
That have been pressed so long
Into a corner of the roof
That they are brown and soft,
And liable to melt as snow.

Over the greatness of such space
Steps must be gentle.
It is all hung by an invisible white hair.
It trembles as birch limbs webbing the air.

And I ask myself:

"Are your fingers long enough to play
Old keys that are but echoes:
Is the silence strong enough

To carry back the music to its source
And back to you again
As though to her?"

Yet I would lead my grandmother by the hand
Through much of what she would not understand;
And so I stumble.   And the rain continues on the
    roof
With such a sound of gently pitying laughter.

# SUNDAY MORNING APPLES

*To William Sommer*

THE leaves will fall again sometime and fill
The fleece of nature with those purposes
That are your rich and faithful strength of line.

But now there are challenges to spring
In that ripe nude with head
       reared
Into a realm of swords, her purple shadow
Bursting on the winter of the world
From whiteness that cries defiance to the snow.

A boy runs with a dog before the sun, straddling
Spontaneities that form their independent orbits,
Their own perennials of light
In the valley where you live
      (called Brandywine).

I have seen the apples there that toss you
  secrets,—
Beloved apples of seasonable madness
That feed your inquiries with aerial wine.

Put them again beside a pitcher with a knife,
And poise them full and ready for explosion—
The apples, Bill, the apples!

# PRAISE FOR AN URN

*In Memoriam: Ernest Nelson*

It was a kind and northern face
That mingled in such exile guise
The everlasting eyes of Pierrot
And, of Gargantua, the laughter.

His thoughts, delivered to me
From the white coverlet and pillow,
I see now, were inheritances—
Delicate riders of the storm.

The slant moon on the slanting hill
Once moved us toward presentiments
Of what the dead keep, living still,
And such assessments of the soul

As, perched in the crematory lobby,
The insistent clock commented on,
Touching as well upon our praise
Of glories proper to the time.

Still, having in mind gold hair,
I cannot see that broken brow
And miss the dry sound of bees
Stretching across a lucid space.

Scatter these well-meant idioms
Into the smoky spring that fills
The suburbs, where they will be lost.
They are no trophies of the sun.

# GARDEN ABSTRACT

THE apple on its bough is her desire,—
Shining suspension, mimic of the sun.
The bough has caught her breath up, and her
    voice,
Dumbly articulate in the slant and rise
Of branch on branch above her, blurs her eyes.
She is prisoner of the tree and its green fingers.

And so she comes to dream herself the tree,
The wind possessing her, weaving her young veins,
Holding her to the sky and its quick blue,
Drowning the fever of her hands in sunlight.
She has no memory, nor fear, nor hope
Beyond the grass and shadows at her feet.

# STARK MAJOR

THE lover's death, how regular
With lifting spring and starker
Vestiges of the sun that somehow
Filter in to us before we waken.

Not yet is there that heat and sober
Vivisection of more clamant air
That hands joined in the dark will answer
After the daily circuits of its glare.

It is the time of sundering . . .
Beneath the green silk counterpane
Her mound of undelivered life
Lies cool upon her—not yet pain.

And she will wake before you pass,
Scarcely aloud, beyond her door,
And every third step down the stair
Until you reach the muffled floor—

Will laugh and call your name; while you
Still answering her faint good-byes,
Will find the street, only to look
At doors and stone with broken eyes.

Walk now, and note the lover's death.
Henceforth her memory is more
Than yours, in cries, in ecstasies
You cannot ever reach to share.

# CHAPLINESQUE

WE make our meek adjustments,
Contented with such random consolations
As the wind deposits
In slithered and too ample pockets.

For we can still love the world, who find
A famished kitten on the step, and know
Recesses for it from the fury of the street,
Or warm torn elbow coverts.

We will sidestep, and to the final smirk
Dally the doom of that inevitable thumb
That slowly chafes its puckered index toward us,
Facing the dull squint with what innocence
And what surprise!

And yet these fine collapses are not lies
More than the pirouettes of any pliant cane;
Our obsequies are, in a way, no enterprise.
We can evade you, and all else but the heart:
What blame to us if the heart live on.

The game enforces smirks; but we have seen
The moon in lonely alleys make
A grail of laughter of an empty ash can,
And through all sound of gaiety and quest
Have heard a kitten in the wilderness.

# PASTORALE

No more violets,
And the year
Broken into smoky panels.
What woods remember now
Her calls, her enthusiasms.

That ritual of sap and leaves
The sun drew out,
Ends in this latter muffled
Bronze and brass.   The wind
Takes rein.

If, dusty, I bear
An image beyond this
Already fallen harvest,
I can only query, "Fool—
Have you remembered too
    long;

Or was there too little said
For ease or resolution—
Summer scarcely begun
And violets,
A few picked, the rest dead?"

# IN SHADOW

Out in the late amber afternoon,
Confused among chrysanthemums,
Her parasol, a pale balloon,
Like a waiting moon, in shadow swims.

Her furtive lace and misty hair
Over the garden dial distill
The sunlight,—then withdrawing, wear
Again the shadows at her will.

Gently yet suddenly, the sheen
Of stars inwraps her parasol.
She hears my step behind the green
Twilight, stiller than shadows, fall.

"Come, it is too late,—too late
To risk alone the light's decline:
Nor has the evening long to wait,"—
But her own words are night's and mine.

# THE FERNERY

The lights that travel on her spectacles
Seldom, now, meet a mirror in her eyes.
But turning, as you may chance to lift a shade
Beside her and her fernery, is to follow
The zigzags fast around dry lips composed
To darkness through a wreath of sudden pain.

—So, while fresh sunlight splinters humid green
I have known myself a nephew to confusions
That sometimes take up residence and reign
In crowns less grey—O merciless tidy hair!

# NORTH LABRADOR

A LAND of leaning ice
Hugged by plaster-grey arches of sky,
Flings itself silently
Into eternity.

"Has no one come here to win you,
Or left you with the faintest blush
Upon your glittering breasts?
Have you no memories, O Darkly Bright?"

Cold-hushed, there is only the shifting of
    moments
That journey toward no Spring—
No birth, no death, no time nor sun
In answer.

# REPOSE OF RIVERS

THE willows carried a slow sound,
A sarabande the wind mowed on the mead.
I could never remember
That seething, steady leveling of the marshes
Till age had brought me to the sea.

Flags, weeds.  And remembrance of steep alcoves
Where cypresses shared the noon's
Tyranny; they drew me into hades almost.
And mammoth turtles climbing sulphur dreams
Yielded, while sun-silt rippled them
Asunder . . .

How much I would have bartered! the black
        gorge
And all the singular nestings in the hills
Where beavers learn stitch and tooth.
The pond I entered once and quickly fled—
I remember now its singing willow rim.

And finally, in that memory all things nurse;
After the city that I finally passed

With scalding unguents spread and smoking
    darts
The monsoon cut across the delta
At gulf gates . . . There, beyond the dykes

I heard wind flaking sapphire, like this summer,
And willows could not hold more steady sound.

# PARAPHRASE

Of a steady winking beat between
Systole, diastole spokes-of-a-wheel
One rushing from the bed at night
May find the record wedged in his soul.

Above the feet the clever sheets
Lie guard upon the integers of life:
For what skims in between uncurls the toe,
Involves the hands in purposeless repose.

But from its bracket how can the tongue tell
When systematic morn shall sometime flood
The pillow—how desperate is the light
That shall not rouse, how faint the crow's cavil

As, when stunned in that antarctic blaze,
Your head, unrocking to a pulse, already
Hollowed by air, posts a white paraphrase
Among bruised roses on the papered wall.

# POSSESSIONS

WITNESS now this trust! the rain
That steals softly direction
And the key, ready to hand—sifting
One moment in sacrifice (the direst)
Through a thousand nights the flesh
Assaults outright for bolts that linger
Hidden,—O undirected as the sky
That through its black foam has no eyes
For this fixed stone of lust . . .

Accumulate such moments to an hour:
Account the total of this trembling tabulation.
I know the screen, the distant flying taps
And stabbing medley that sways—
And the mercy, feminine, that stays
As though prepared.

And I, entering, take up the stone
As quiet as you can make a man . . .
In Bleecker Street, still trenchant in a void,
Wounded by apprehensions out of speech,

I hold it up against a disk of light—
I, turning, turning on smoked forking spires,
The city's stubborn lives, desires.

Tossed on these horns, who bleeding dies,
Lacks all but piteous admissions to be spilt
Upon the page whose blind sum finally burns
Record of rage and partial appetites.
The pure possession, the inclusive cloud
Whose heart is fire shall come,—the white wind
    rase
All but bright stones wherein our smiling plays.

# LACHRYMAE CHRISTI

WHITELY, while benzine
Rinsings from the moon
Dissolve all but the windows of the mills
(Inside the sure machinery
Is still
And curdled only where a sill
Sluices its one unyielding smile)

Immaculate venom binds
The fox's teeth, and swart
Thorns freshen on the year's
First blood.  From flanks unfended,
Twanged red perfidies of spring
Are trillion on the hill.

And the nights opening
Chant pyramids,—
Anoint with innocence,—recall
To music and retrieve what perjuries
Had galvanized the eyes.

While chime
Beneath and all around
Distilling clemencies,—worms'
Inaudible whistle, tunneling
Not penitence
But song, as these
Perpetual fountains, vines,—


Thy Nazarene and tinder eyes.


(Let sphinxes from the ripe
Borage of death have cleared my tongue
Once and again; vermin and rod
No longer bind.  Some sentient cloud
Of tears flocks through the tendoned loam:
Betrayed stones slowly speak.)


Names peeling from Thine eyes
And their undimming lattices of flame,
Spell out in palm and pain
Compulsion of the year, O Nazarene.


Lean long from sable, slender boughs,
Unstanched and luminous.  And as the nights
Strike from Thee perfect spheres,
Lift up in lilac-emerald breath the grail
Of earth again—

                    Thy face
From charred and riven stakes, O
Dionysus, Thy
Unmangled target smile,

# PASSAGE

WHERE the cedar leaf divides the sky
I heard the sea.
In sapphire arenas of the hills
I was promised an improved infancy.

Sulking, sanctioning the sun,
My memory I left in a ravine,—
Casual louse that tissues the buckwheat,
Aprons rocks, congregates pears
In moonlit bushels
And wakens alleys with a hidden cough.

Dangerously the summer burned
(I had joined the entrainments of the wind).
The shadows of boulders lengthened my back:
In the bronze gongs of my cheeks
The rain dried without odour.

"It is not long, it is not long;
See where the red and black
Vine-stanchioned valleys—": but the wind
Died speaking through the ages that you know

And hug, chimney-sooted heart of man!
So was I turned about and back, much as your smoke
Compiles a too well known biography.

The evening was a spear in the ravine
That throve through very oak.   And had I walked
The dozen particular decimals of time?
Touching an opening laurel, I found
A thief beneath, my stolen book in hand.

"Why are you back here—smiling an iron coffin?"
"To argue with the laurel," I replied:
"Am justified in transience, fleeing
Under the constant wonder of your eyes—."

He closed the book.   And from the Ptolemies
Sand troughed us in a glittering abyss.
A serpent swam a vertex to the sun
—On unpaced beaches leaned its tongue and drummed.
What fountains did I hear? what icy speeches?
Memory, committed to the page, had broke.

# THE WINE MENAGERIE

INVARIABLY when wine redeems the sight,
Narrowing the mustard scansions of the eyes,
A leopard ranging always in the brow
Asserts a vision in the slumbering gaze.

Then glozening decanters that reflect the street
Wear me in crescents on their bellies.  Slow
Applause flows into liquid cynosures:
—I am conscripted to their shadows' glow.


Against the imitation onyx wainscoting
(Painted emulsion of snow, eggs, yarn, coal,
     manure)
Regard the forceps of the smile that takes her.
Percussive sweat is spreading to his hair.
     Mallets,
Her eyes, unmake an instant of the world . . .

What is it in this heap the serpent pries—
Whose skin, facsimile of time, unskeins

Octagon, sapphire transepts round the eyes;
—From whom some whispered carillon assures
Speed to the arrow into feathered skies?

Sharp to the windowpane guile drags a face,
And as the alcove of her jealousy recedes
An urchin who has left the snow
Nudges a cannister across the bar
While August meadows somewhere clasp his
    brow.

Each chamber, transept, coins some squint,
Remorseless line, minting their separate wills—
Poor streaked bodies wreathing up and out,
Unwitting the stigma that each turn repeals:
Between black tusks the roses shine!

New thresholds, new anatomies! Wine talons
Build freedom up about me and distill
This competence—to travel in a·tear
Sparkling alone, within another's will.

Until my blood dreams a receptive smile
Wherein new purities are snared; where chimes
Before some flame of gaunt repose a shell
Tolled once, perhaps, by every tongue in hell.
—Anguished, the wit that cries out of me:

"Alas,—these frozen billows of your skill!
Invent new dominoes of love and bile . . .

Ruddy, the tooth implicit of the world
Has followed you.  Though in the end you know
And count some dim inheritance of sand,
How much yet meets the treason of the snow.

"Rise from the dates and crumbs.  And walk away,
Stepping over Holofernes' shins—
Beyond the wall, whose severed head floats by
With Baptist John's.  Their whispering begins.

"—And fold your exile on your back again;
Petrushka's valentine pivots on its pin."

# RECITATIVE

REGARD the capture here, O Janus-faced,
As double as the hands that twist this glass.
Such eyes at search or rest you cannot see;
Reciting pain or glee, how can you bear!

Twin shadowed halves: the breaking second holds
In each the skin alone, and so it is
I crust a plate of vibrant mercury
Borne cleft to you, and brother in the half.

Inquire this much-exacting fragment smile,
Its drums and darkest blowing leaves ignore,—
Defer though, revocation of the tears
That yield attendance to one crucial sign.

Look steadily—how the wind feasts and spins
The brain's disk shivered against lust.    Then
        watch
While darkness, like an ape's face, falls away,
And gradually white buildings answer day.

Let the same nameless gulf beleaguer us—
Alike suspend us from atrocious sums
Built floor by floor on shafts of steel that grant
The plummet heart, like Absalom, no stream.

The highest tower,—let her ribs palisade
Wrenched gold of Nineveh;—yet leave the tower.
The bridge swings over salvage, beyond wharves;
A wind abides the ensign of your will . . .

In alternating bells have you not heard
All hours clapped dense into a single stride?
Forgive me for an echo of these things,
And let us walk through time with equal pride.

# FOR THE MARRIAGE OF FAUSTUS AND HELEN

*"And so we may arrive by Talmud skill*
*And profane Greek to raise the building up*
*Of Helen's house against the Ismaelite,*
*King of Thogarma, and his habergeons*
*Brimstony, blue and fiery; and the force*
*Of King Abaddon, and the beast of Cittim;*
*Which Rabbi David Kimchi, Onkelos,*
*And Aben Ezra do interpret Rome."*
—THE ALCHEMIST.

## I

THE mind has shown itself at times
Too much the baked and labeled dough
Divided by accepted multitudes.
Across the stacked partitions of the day—
Across the memoranda, baseball scores,
The stenographic smiles and stock quotations
Smutty wings flash out equivocations.

The mind is brushed by sparrow wings;
Numbers, rebuffed by asphalt, crowd
The margins of the day, accent the curbs,
Convoying divers dawns on every corner
To druggist, barber and tobacconist,
Until the graduate opacities of evening
Take them away as suddenly to somewhere
Virginal perhaps, less fragmentary, cool.

>   *There is the world dimensional for*
>   *those untwisted by the love of things*
>   *irreconcilable . . .*

And yet, suppose some evening I forgot
The fare and transfer, yet got by that way
Without recall,—lost yet poised in traffic.
Then I might find your eyes across an aisle,
Still flickering with those prefigurations—
Prodigal, yet uncontested now,
Half-riant before the jerky window frame.

There is some way, I think, to touch
Those hands of yours that count the nights
Stippled with pink and green advertisements.
And now, before its arteries turn dark
I would have you meet this bartered blood.
Imminent in his dream, none better knows
The white wafer cheek of love, or offers words
Lightly as moonlight on the eaves meets snow.

Reflective conversion of all things
At your deep blush, when ecstasies thread
The limbs and belly, when rainbows spread
Impinging on the throat and sides . . .
Inevitable, the body of the world
Weeps in inventive dust for the hiatus
That winks above it, bluet in your breasts.

The earth may glide diaphanous to death;
But if I lift my arms it is to bend
To you who turned away once, Helen, knowing
The press of troubled hands, too alternate
With steel and soil to hold you endlessly.
I meet you, therefore, in that eventual flame
You found in final chains, no captive then—
Beyond their million brittle, bloodshot eyes;
White, through white cities passed on to assume
That world which comes to each of us alone.

Accept a lone eye riveted to your plane,
Bent axle of devotion along companion ways
That beat, continuous, to hourless days—
One inconspicuous, glowing orb of praise.

## II

Brazen hypnotics glitter here;
Glee shifts from foot to foot,
Magnetic to their tremulo.
This crashing opera bouffe,
Blest excursion! this ricochet
From roof to roof—
Know, Olympians, we are breathless
While nigger cupids scour the stars!

A thousand light shrugs balance us
Through snarling hails of melody.
White shadows slip across the floor
Splayed like cards from a loose hand;
Rhythmic ellipses lead into canters
Until somewhere a rooster banters.

Greet naïvely—yet intrepidly
New soothings, new amazements
That cornets introduce at every turn—
And you may fall downstairs with me
With perfect grace and equanimity.
Or, plaintively scud past shores
Where, by strange harmonic laws
All relatives, serene and cool,
Sit rocked in patent armchairs.

O, I have known metallic paradises
Where cuckoos clucked to finches
Above the deft catastrophes of drums.
While titters hailed the groans of death
Beneath gyrating awnings I have seen
The incunabula of the divine grotesque.
This music has a reassuring way.

The siren of the springs of guilty song—
Let us take her on the incandescent wax
Striated with nuances, nervosities
That we are heir to: she is still so young,
We cannot frown upon her as she smiles,
Dipping here in this cultivated storm
Among slim skaters of the gardened skies.

# III

Capped arbiter of beauty in this street
That narrows darkly into motor dawn,—
You, here beside me, delicate ambassador
Of intricate slain numbers that arise
In whispers, naked of steel;

                                 religious gunman!
Who faithfully, yourself, will fall too soon,
And in other ways than as the wind settles
On the sixteen thrifty bridges of the city:
Let us unbind our throats of fear and pity.

                                 We even,
Who drove speediest destruction
In corymbulous formations of mechanics,—
Who hurried the hill breezes, spouting malice
Plangent over meadows, and looked down
On rifts of torn and empty houses
Like old women with teeth unjubilant
That waited faintly, briefly and in vain:

We know, eternal gunman, our flesh remembers
The tensile boughs, the nimble blue plateaus,
The mounted, yielding cities of the air!

That saddled sky that shook down vertical
Repeated play of fire—no hypogeum
Of wave or rock was good against one hour.
We did not ask for that, but have survived,
And will persist to speak again before
All stubble streets that have not curved
To memory, or known the ominous lifted arm
That lowers down the arc of Helen's brow
To saturate with blessing and dismay.


A goose, tobacco and cologne—
Three winged and gold-shod prophecies of
        heaven,
The lavish heart shall always have to leaven
And spread with bells and voices, and atone
The abating shadows of our conscript dust.


Anchises' navel, dripping of the sea,—
The hands Erasmus dipped in gleaming tides,
Gathered the voltage of blown blood and vine;
Delve upward for the new and scattered wine,
O brother-thief of time, that we recall.
Laugh out the meager penance of their days
Who dare not share with us the breath released,
The substance drilled and spent beyond repair
For golden, or the shadow of gold hair.

Distinctly praise the years, whose volatile
Blamed bleeding hands extend and thresh the
    height
The imagination spans beyond despair,
Outpacing bargain, vocable and prayer.

# AT MELVILLE'S TOMB

OFTEN beneath the wave, wide from this ledge
The dice of drowned men's bones he saw bequeath
An embassy.  Their numbers as he watched,
Beat on the dusty shore and were obscured.

And wrecks passed without sound of bells,
The calyx of death's bounty giving back
A scattered chapter, livid hieroglyph,
The portent wound in corridors of shells.

Then in the circuit calm of one vast coil,
Its lashings charmed and malice reconciled,
Frosted eyes there were that lifted altars;
And silent answers crept across the stars.

Compass, quadrant and sextant contrive
No farther tides . . . High in the azure steeps
Monody shall not wake the mariner.
This fabulous shadow only the sea keeps.

# VOYAGES

# VOYAGES

## I

ABOVE the fresh ruffles of the surf
Bright striped urchins flay each other with sand.
They have contrived a conquest for shell shucks,
And their fingers crumble fragments of baked
     weed
Gaily digging and scattering.

And in answer to their treble interjections
The sun beats lightning on the waves,
The waves fold thunder on the sand;
And could they hear me I would tell them:

O brilliant kids, frisk with your dog,
Fondle your shells and sticks, bleached
By time and the elements; but there is a line
You must not cross nor ever trust beyond it
Spry cordage of your bodies to caresses
Too lichen-faithful from too wide a breast.
The bottom of the sea is cruel.

## II

—And yet this great wink of eternity,
Of rimless floods, unfettered leewardings,
Samite sheeted and processioned where
Her undinal vast belly moonward bends,
Laughing the wrapt inflections of our love;

Take this Sea, whose diapason knells
On scrolls of silver snowy sentences,
The sceptred terror of whose sessions rends
As her demeanors motion well or ill,
All but the pieties of lovers' hands.

And onward, as bells off San Salvador
Salute the crocus lustres of the stars,
In these poinsettia meadows of her tides,—
Adagios of islands, O my Prodigal,
Complete the dark confessions her veins spell.

Mark how her turning shoulders wind the hours,
And hasten while her penniless rich palms
Pass superscription of bent foam and wave,—
Hasten, while they are true,—sleep, death, desire,
Close round one instant in one floating flower.

Bind us in time, O Seasons clear, and awe.
O minstrel galleons of Carib fire,
Bequeath us to no earthly shore until
Is answered in the vortex of our grave
The seal's wide spindrift gaze toward paradise.

# III

Infinite consanguinity it bears—
This tendered theme of you that light
Retrieves from sea plains where the sky
Resigns a breast that every wave enthrones;
While ribboned water lanes I wind
Are laved and scattered with no stroke
Wide from your side, whereto this hour
The sea lifts, also, reliquary hands.

And so, admitted through black swollen gates
That must arrest all distance otherwise,—
Past whirling pillars and lithe pediments,
Light wrestling there incessantly with light,
Star kissing star through wave on wave unto
Your body rocking!
           and where death, if shed,
Presumes no carnage, but this single change,—
Upon the steep floor flung from dawn to dawn
The silken skilled transmemberment of song;

Permit me voyage, love, into your hands . . .

## IV

Whose counted smile of hours and days, suppose
I know as spectrum of the sea and pledge
Vastly now parting gulf on gulf of wings
Whose circles bridge, I know, (from palms to the
    severe
Chilled albatross's white immutability)
No stream of greater love advancing now
Than, singing, this mortality alone
Through clay aflow immortally to you.

All fragrance irrefragibly, and claim
Madly meeting logically in this hour
And region that is ours to wreathe again,
Portending eyes and lips and making told
The chancel port and portion of our June—

Shall they not stem and close in our own steps
Bright staves of flowers and quills to-day as I
Must first be lost in fatal tides to tell?

In signature of the incarnate word
The harbor shoulders to resign in mingling
Mutual blood, transpiring as foreknown
And widening noon within your breast for
    gathering
All bright insinuations that my years have caught
For islands where must lead inviolably
Blue latitudes and levels of your eyes,—

In this expectant, still exclaim receive
The secret oar and petals of all love.

# V

Meticulous, past midnight in clear rime,
Infrangible and lonely, smooth as though cast
Together in one merciless white blade—
The bay estuaries fleck the hard sky limits.

—As if too brittle or too clear to touch!
The cables of our sleep so swiftly filed,
Already hang, shred ends from remembered stars.
One frozen trackless smile. . . What words
Can strangle this deaf moonlight? For we

Are overtaken. Now no cry, no sword
Can fasten or deflect this tidal wedge,
Slow tyranny of moonlight, moonlight loved
And changed . . . "There's

Nothing like this in the world," you say,
Knowing I cannot touch your hand and look
Too, into that godless cleft of sky
Where nothing turns but dead sands flashing.

"—And never to quite understand!"   No,
In all the argosy of your bright hair I dreamed
Nothing so flagless as this piracy.

                              But now
Draw in your head, alone and too tall here.
Your eyes already in the slant of drifting foam;
Your breath sealed by the ghosts I do not know:
Draw in your head and sleep the long way home.

## VI

Where icy and bright dungeons lift
Of swimmers their lost morning eyes,
And ocean rivers, churning, shift
Green borders under stranger skies,

Steadily as a shell secretes
Its beating leagues of monotone,
Or as many waters trough the sun's
Red kelson past the cape's wet stone;

O rivers mingling toward the sky
And harbor of the phœnix' breast—
My eyes pressed black against the prow,
—Thy derelict and blinded guest

Waiting, afire, what name, unspoke,
I cannot claim: let thy waves rear
More savage than the death of kings,
Some splintered garland for the seer.

Beyond siroccos harvesting
The solstice thunders, crept away,
Like a cliff swinging or a sail
Flung into April's inmost day—

Creation's blithe and petalled word
To the lounged goddess when she rose
Conceding dialogue with eyes
That smile unsearchable repose—

Still fervid covenant, Belle Isle,
—Unfolded floating dais before
Which rainbows twine continual hair—
Belle Isle, white echo of the oar!

The imaged Word, it is, that holds
Hushed willows anchored in its glow.
It is the unbetrayable reply
Whose accent no farewell can know.